P9-EME-485

Debby Ryan

Her Sweet Life!

By Riley Brooks

SCHOLASTIC INC.

New York   Toronto   London   Auckland
Sydney   Mexico City   New Delhi   Hong Kong

Photo Credits: cover: © David Livingston/Getty Images; pg. 1: © Michael Bezjian/Wirelmage; pg. 4: © Peter Brooker/Rex USA; pg. 6: Byron Purvis/AdMedia/Newscom; pg. 8: © Jesse Grant/Wirelmage; pg. 10: © Gabriel Bouys/AFP/Getty Images; pg. 12: © Michael Buckner/Getty Images; pg 13: © Jeffrey Mayer/ Wirelmage; pg. 14: © Charles Eshelman/ FilmMagic/ Getty Images; pg 17: Michael Germana/Globe Photos/ Newscom; pg. 18: © Ken Babolcay-IPOL-Globe Photos/ Newscom; pg. 20: © Jen Lowery / Splash News; pg. 23: © Bauer-Griffin; pg. 24: © Leigh Vogel/Getty Images; pg. 26: © Michael Bezjian/Wirelmage; pg. 27: © Jen Lowery / Splash News; pg. 29: © Todd Williamson/Wirelmage; pg. 30: © Scott Mitchell/ZUMA Press; back cover: © Frazer Harrison/Getty Images.

No part of this work may be reproduced in whole or in part, stored in a retrieval system, or transmitted in any form or by any means, electronic, mechanical, photocopying, recording, or other- wise, without written permission of the publisher. For information regarding permission, write to Scholastic Inc., Attention: Permissions Department, 557 Broadway, New York, NY 10012.

© 2010 by Scholastic
ISBN 978-0-545-29637-3

Published by Scholastic Inc.
SCHOLASTIC and associated logos are trademarks and/or registered trademarks of Scholastic Inc.

12 11 10 9 8 7 6 5 4 3 2 1   10 11 12 13 14 15/0

Printed in the U.S.A.   40
First printing, September 2010

Table of Contents

Introduction

Have you ever wondered what it would be like to star in a TV show? Or to work with two super-cute twin brothers? Hang out with the coolest stars at parties and premieres? It would be pretty sweet, right?

Well, get ready to find out! Because today's newest star Debby Ryan does all those things and more! This book is filled with everything about Debby—from her childhood start in Germany to her current gig as a Disney darling. It's almost as good as being on set with Debby!

Chapter 1 · Little Debby

Debby has a pretty sweet life now, but before she was a famous actress, she was just an average girl in Huntsville, Alabama. Deborah Ann Ryan made her debut into the world on May 13, 1993. Her father, Chris, worked for the U.S. Army, and

her mother, Sandy, was a stay-at-home mom. Her parents were thrilled to have a baby girl, but it was probably her older brother Chase who was most excited to have a sister.

Debby grew up as a bubbly child. Her family was active at their church, and she went to a small private school. But when Debby was seven years old, she and her family moved to Germany. Debby and her brother became best friends during their time abroad. At first, it was difficult to fit in at their German school because they didn't speak German. But both of them became fluent pretty quickly!

Debby's parents encouraged both kids to get involved in activities to help them adjust to their new home. Debby decided to try out for a few theater productions at an American theater in town. It was the perfect fit for her. "When I moved to Germany at seven years old, I got involved in professional American theater. I would

go to the theater straight from school and usually stay late, finishing my homework and studying in between my scenes," Debby explained on www. debbyryan.com. Debby loved acting, and her parents were proud of her performances. It was clear the Ryans had a star on their hands.

After three years, the Ryan family moved back to the U.S.A.—this time to a small town named Keller, Texas. Debby was sad to leave Germany, but she was also excited to start middle school. Of course, Texas was really different from Germany. Debby didn't have the easiest time fitting in. She joined the school's theater productions and the chess club, but some of the popular girls picked on Debby for her "nerdy" hobbies. It was a rough time for Debby. She had her brother to lean on, but she missed having a big group of friends. She knew she needed to do something that made her happy outside of school. So Debby decided to pursue professional acting. "I realized that unless acting played a significant role in my life, I wasn't happy," Debby explained on www.debbyryan.com. She had no idea just how far that decision would take her!

Chapter 2 · There Are No Small Parts

When Debby told her family she wanted to become a professional actress, they were very supportive. Her mom helped Debby find a great agent and she began auditioning. Debby explained, "My first audition was for a small teenage spot on a *Barney* film, and I booked it!" Debby was super excited for her first real role.

She played a teenager in 2007's *Barney: Let's Go to the Firehouse*, a direct-to-video Barney special about fire safety. Debby had a great time working with the iconic purple dinosaur. She was proud of her first accomplishment as a pro and was ready for more!

Next, Debby booked two national commercials. The first was for the iDog Amp'd, a robotic dog toy that was also a speaker for iPods. The iDog moved, barked, and danced along to the music from the iPod. Next she starred in a commercial for "The Game of Life: Twists and Turns," a new take on the classic board game. It was pretty amazing to see herself on TV, and to know that people across the country were watching her commercials.

Around that time, Debby sent in a video audition to the Disney Channel. She knew it would probably be a while before they heard anything back, so Debby continued to go on auditions.

Then Debby scored a role that she was excited about. It was a small part in a feature film called *The Longshots*. *The Longshots* starred fellow teen actress Keke Palmer as a girl who wanted to play football with the boys. Debby played Edith, the film's mean girl. Debby's such a sweetheart that it was tough for her to play a mean girl, but it was fun to pretend! It was also fun seeing the movie up on the big screen when it premiered. At the time, Debby didn't think it could get any better. Little did she know that the best was yet to come!

Chapter 3 · Debby on Deck

A few months later, Debby got a call from her agent letting her know that Disney liked her video audition. They flew Debby and her mom all the way to Hollywood for a screen test. Disney was looking for someone to play the innocent farm girl Bailey Pickett on *The Suite Life on Deck*, a spin-off of the popular Disney show *The Suite Life of Zack and Cody*. In the new show, Zack, Cody, and

London Tipton set sail on a luxury cruise ship called the *S.S. Tipton* to attend Seven Seas High. Mr. Moseby manages the boat. Bailey Pickett is a student at Seven Seas High that Cody has a huge crush on. Talk about a great role!

It was a long audition process, but it was worth it! Debby explained on www.debbyryan.com: "After a nerve-racking screen test and a long six days of waiting and hoping, I got a phone call that changed my life!" Disney wanted Debby to play

Bailey! Once she received the good news, Debby and her mom had only a week to pack up and make the move to Los Angeles. They had to leave Debby's dad and brother behind until they could move out and join them. It was hard on the family to be separated, but they never complained. Everyone was so proud of Debby that they didn't mind making the sacrifice.

Debby was a little star-struck her first day on set. After all, she'd been watching Cole Sprouse, Dylan Sprouse, and Brenda Song on TV for years! But everyone made her feel right at home. Getting into character definitely helped her get settled. Debby saw some of herself in Bailey! "We are both strong and independent and not afraid to roll our sleeves up," Debby told *The Glendale News Press*. "I love school, and we both like learning and bettering ourselves. And she's a little nicer than I am."

On September 26, 2008, the first episode

of *The Suite Life on Deck* aired. Millions of fans tuned in. It was a hit!

Debby has become good friends with her co-stars, and she always has a great time on set, as she explained to justjaredjr.com. "My favorite place to hang out on set is the Juice Bar, it's so cool! And there's the spiral staircase on the show with chairs under it. We all sit there and talk, I love it! I like showing people around, too. There are different alcoves and secret passageways!"

Debby loves her job. She's gotten to film a lot of cool scenes for the show. One of her favorites was a special crossover episode where the stars of *Wizards of Waverly Place* and *Hannah Montana* sailed on the *S.S. Tipton.* Debby and her co-stars had a blast working with other Disney stars, including Miley Cyrus, Emily Osment, Selena Gomez, and David Henrie. In one episode, Debby even got to kiss Cole Sprouse when their characters started dating. How lucky is she?

Chapter 4 · The Disney Life

As a *Suite Life* star, Debby became part of the Disney family! As part of the family, Debby has participated in lots of Disney projects. She filmed promotions, gave interviews for *Disney 365* and *Radio Disney*, and guest starred on other Disney programs and specials. She even made a special video diary of her first few weeks as a Disney darling.

Debby got to make a cameo appearance in *Jonas Brothers: Living the Dream*. It was a special all about the behind-the-scenes lives of Nick, Joe, and Kevin Jonas. Debby has always been a big Jo Bro fan, so she was thrilled to meet the boys!

Debby also appeared on the first show of *Studio DC: Almost Live*, that starred the Muppets and lots of Disney Channel stars. It was pretty

cool working with the Muppets. After all, there aren't that many people who can claim they've met Kermit up close and personal!

When Disney discovered that Debby could sing, they asked her to record a song for *Disney-Mania 7*. Debby was flattered. She chose to sing "Hakuna Matata" from *The Lion King* because it's always been one of her favorite Disney songs. "I love 'Hakuna Matata'—I even have a toothbrush that sings it to me. My best friend gave it to me!" Debby revealed to justjaredjr.com. Getting to have a song on an album alongside major Disney stars such as Selena Gomez, Demi Lovato, and Mitchell Musso was a dream come true for Debby!

Of course, the best part of being in the Disney family is getting to go to Disney parties and premieres. Debby loves walking the red carpet— and she always looks super stylish doing so. Being part of the Disney family is pretty sweet!

Chapter 5 · Made for TV

As much as Debby loves working on her TV show, she also enjoys the challenge of taking on movie roles. Since filming *The Longshots*, Debby has starred in two independent films: *What If...* and *16 Wishes*.

Debby filmed *What If...* in July 2009. "I managed to fit in the small role [of] Kimberly on an independent family film *What If...* on my week off. I got to work with Kevin Sorbo and Kristy Swanson, who play my parents," Debby told fans on www.debbyryan.com. It is a dramatic film about family and faith. Debby's role was a little tough. She had to be able to cry on demand! Director Dallas Jenkins was pleased with her acting skills. As he told susiemagazine.com: "Even in scenes where she had to cry or laugh, she didn't overdo it or push it. That's very rare in a young actor. After her first scene, I knew I was going to love her performance." *What If...* released directly to DVD. Debby was thrilled to be involved in a project that highlighted her faith.

Debby's next independent project was the made-for-television movie *16 Wishes*, a story about a girl named Abby, played by Debby, who

gets sixteen magical wishes for her sixteenth birthday. Abby has a list of sixteen things she wants to accomplish. On the morning of her sweet sixteen, a birthday fairy appears and gives Abby sixteen numbered candles. Every time Abby lights a candle, her corresponding wish from the list comes true. It's great at first, until one wish backfires, and Abby thinks she may have lost her friends forever. Of course, the movie has a happy ending!

Filming *16 Wishes* was fun, especially when it came time for the scenes with magic in them! Debby got to drive a super-cool car, wear amazing clothes, and even flirt with her adorable co-stars! The best part for Debby, though, was meeting Jean-Luc Bilodeau, one of the stars of Debby's favorite TV show *Kyle XY*. Jean-Luc played Abby's best friend. Debby became great friends with all of her co-stars. They had a blast filming together, especially the party scenes!

16 Wishes premiered on the Disney Channel in June 2010. Everyone loved the movie. Hopefully, Debby will star in another movie soon, because her fans just can't get enough of her!

Chapter 6 · Making Music

The only thing Debby loves as much as acting is music. She adores everything about music—listening to it, writing it, and performing it! Debby plays the guitar, piano, and keyboard,

and writes songs. Debby is a big fan of lots of different genres of music, so it's been difficult for her to pick one sound to focus on. "I love jazz! I love singing it. I also love country! My brother loves rock; he also has this chill Jason Mraz-like style... But I honestly would love to make country music," Debby told *People* magazine. She's written her first single, a song called "Adiós," and is waiting for the perfect time to release it.

Disney has given Debby a chance to develop her musical talents, but she hasn't signed a recording contract yet. She performed a song as Bailey on an episode of *The Suite Life on Deck* called "Beauty and the Fleeced." Then she recorded the cover of "Hakuna Matata" for *Disney-Mania 7*.

Debby is excited about launching a music career, but she's not in any hurry. Luckily, she has plenty of time to do all of that and keep acting, because her career is just starting!

Chapter 7 · Behind the Camera

So what is life like for Debby when she's not working? Pretty normal! She counts her co-stars, Cole, Dylan, and Brenda as some of her best friends in Los Angeles. All of Debby's co-

stars and other industry friends came out for her super-fun sweet sixteen birthday party. It had a masquerade theme, and everyone wore beautiful masks. Debby actually collects masks, so she was thrilled to show hers off!

Debby takes dance classes and loves to go horseback riding. "I'm super close to the equestrian center and go riding with my friends. Riding is peaceful, passive, and gentle. I [also] took

classes in ballet, jazz, and drill team at high school. I incorporate everything with hip-hop," Debby explained to www.justjaredjr.com. Debby has already finished high school and is taking online college courses.

But Debby's main hobby is music. She loves pairing the perfect song with everything she does! Debby told *Relate Magazine* that she likes "...finding new independent artists that make music on a computer, in coffee houses, that are as equally talented as big names in the industry. It is like my personal treasure hunt." Debby even writes a music blog on www.debbyryan.com so she can share her finds with her fans!

Debby considers her brother to be her best friend. She loves hanging with her family, especially on Sundays when they all go to church and have dinner together. She relies on her faith to keep her grounded, no matter what the future holds!

Chapter 8 · Future Wishes

So what's next for this Hollywood sweet-heart?! Debby is hoping to play Bailey on *The Suite Life on Deck* for as long as possible and to film roles in more movies in her downtime. But she's being picky about which parts she accepts. Debby wants to choose roles that she feels will make a difference for her fans. "My long-term goal for acting is to do one movie that profoundly changes people's minds on things. I want it to be a movie that gets in your head, you can't shake it. I want to do an inspirational movie that isn't

cheesy or dark," Debby explained to *Relate Magazine*. Of course, don't rule TV out for Deb. She's totally open to doing another show after *The Suite Life* ends.

Debby loves writing. She wrote on www.debbyryan.com that, "I am writing a screenplay in my off time that I want to one day produce and co-direct... I am developing a fun pilot that I really would love to one day produce. It's still early in the stages of development." It's a safe bet that Debby would be just as great behind the camera as she is in front of it!

There is definitely music in Debby's future. She would love to record a country album someday. Maybe Chase will produce it for her! Debby loves sharing her fav songs on her music blog. So look forward to many more posts to come.

With her talent and great personality, Debby is sure to be successful no matter what she does in the future!

Chapter 9

Full: Deborah Ann Ryan

Birthday: May 13, 1993

Hometown: Keller, Texas

Parents: Chris and Sandy Ryan

Siblings: older brother Chase Ryan

Pets: a cat named Isaac and a Yorkshire terrier named Daisy

Best Friend: her brother Chase

Instruments: guitar, keyboard

Favorite Food: smoothies

Favorite Candy: Milky Way bars

Favorite Shoes: Tom's flats

Favorite Store: Target

Favorite TV Show: *Kyle XY*

Favorite Color: blue

Biggest Collection: masquerade masks